PETRUS W LIEBENBERG

Landing Your First QA Job

A Guide for Career Changers

Copyright © 2024 by Petrus W Liebenberg

All rights reserved. No part of this publication may be reproduced, stored or transmitted in any form or by any means, electronic, mechanical, photocopying, recording, scanning, or otherwise without written permission from the publisher. It is illegal to copy this book, post it to a website, or distribute it by any other means without permission.

First edition

*This book was professionally typeset on Reedsy.
Find out more at reedsy.com*

Contents

1	Introduction	1
2	Chapter 1: Deciding to Transition into Quality Assurance	3
	Understanding the QA Profession	3
	The Career Change Mindset	6
3	Chapter 2: Acquiring QA Knowledge and Skills	9
	Learning the Fundamentals of QA	9
	Hands-On Practice	12
4	Chapter 3: Landing Your First QA Job	16
	Preparing to Apply	16
	Nailing the Interview	19
5	Chapter 4: Growing into a QA Manager Role	23
	Excelling in Your First QA Job	23
	Developing Leadership Skills	26
	Stepping into QA Management	29
6	Conclusion	33

1

Introduction

Welcome to Landing Your First QA Job: A Guide for Career Changers.

If you're reading this, chances are you're at a crossroads in your career. Maybe you're stuck in a job that doesn't challenge you, or perhaps you've been laid off and are wondering, What's next? Or, maybe you're simply ready for something new—something meaningful that offers growth, stability, and a sense of purpose.

Whatever brought you here, know this: a career in Quality Assurance (QA) could be your next big move. And no, you don't need a degree in computer science or decades of tech experience to break in. What you do need is the right mindset, a plan, and the willingness to learn—and that's exactly what this book will give you.

Why QA, and Why Now?

Quality Assurance isn't just about finding bugs in software; it's about making sure products—whether apps, games, or websites—work the way they should. It's the ultimate mix of problem-solving, creativity, and precision. And here's the kicker: QA is one of the few tech roles where transferable skills from other industries are not just welcome but often a competitive advantage.

QA professionals are in demand across industries, from startups to multinational corporations. With the rise of Agile, DevOps, and AI-powered testing, companies need smart, detail-oriented people like you to help them deliver high-quality products.

Your Journey Starts Now

Changing careers can feel daunting. Trust me, I've been there. But it can also be one of the most empowering decisions you'll ever make. The fact that you picked up this book means you're already taking the first step toward a more fulfilling career.

So let's roll up our sleeves and get to work. By the end of this book, you won't just know how to land your first QA job—you'll have a clear roadmap to a thriving career. You've got this.

Turn the page, and let's begin.

2

Chapter 1: Deciding to Transition into Quality Assurance

Understanding the QA Profession

What is QA and Why Does it Matter?

Quality Assurance, or QA, is a term you've probably heard but might not fully understand. At its core, QA is about ensuring that something—whether it's a software application, a physical product, or even a service—meets a set of predefined quality standards. It's not just about catching mistakes; it's about preventing them in the first place. Think of QA as a process of asking, "Does this do what it's supposed to do? And does it do it well?" It's proactive rather than reactive, focused on building reliability and trust into the product from the start.

Now, you might wonder how QA differs from Quality Control (QC) or testing. Here's a simple way to think about it. QA sets the rules of the game—it's about processes, planning, and making sure the conditions for success are in place. QC is the referee, checking the outcome to see if it meets expectations. Testing is a specific tool used in QA to ensure that every function, button, or workflow behaves as it should. QA, QC, and testing work together, but QA holds the big picture.

QA's importance isn't limited to the tech industry. Whether in communications, healthcare, manufacturing, or food production, QA is the backbone of trust between a company and its customers. For software, QA ensures seamless user experiences, reduces costly errors, and builds customer loyalty. It's a profession that's quietly but critically shaping the world around us—and now, perhaps, your future too.

Benefits of a Career in QA

A career in Quality Assurance is like stepping into a field where curiosity meets opportunity. The demand for QA professionals is booming, and it's not hard to see why. Every company relying on technology—essentially all of them—needs someone to ensure their software works flawlessly. Whether it's a startup launching the next big app or a multinational corporation maintaining critical systems, QA professionals are the ones keeping the wheels turning. This demand translates into growing job opportunities that aren't going away anytime soon.

But QA isn't just about getting a foot in the door; it's about building a path for growth. You might start with manual testing, gaining a foundational understanding of how systems work. From there, the possibilities open up. You could dive into automation testing, performance testing, or even niche fields like security testing. With time, some choose leadership roles, guiding teams as QA managers or strategists. The career ladder is there—you just need to decide how high you want to climb.

What's equally appealing is the balance many QA roles offer. Unlike some tech positions that demand endless hours of coding, QA often provides structure and predictability. Many companies embrace remote work or flexible schedules, letting you tailor your day to fit life's other priorities.

Is QA the Right Fit for You?

Before diving headfirst into a QA career, it's worth pausing to reflect—does this path align with who you are and what you enjoy doing? QA is a role for the curious and detail-oriented, the people who love asking "What if?" and thrive on uncovering hidden issues. It's about spotting patterns, thinking critically, and finding satisfaction in solving problems others might overlook. Communication also plays a huge role. Whether you're collaborating with developers, project managers, or stakeholders, being able to explain what's working—and what's not—is a key skill.

At the same time, QA isn't for everyone, and that's okay. Think about how you feel about repetitive tasks or methodical processes. Manual testing, for example, requires patience and precision as you follow test cases step by step. Does that sound satisfying or stifling? QA also demands resilience. Finding flaws can sometimes feel like swimming upstream, especially when tight deadlines or differing opinions come into play.

That said, the rewards can far outweigh the challenges. QA offers variety, intellectual stimulation, and the chance to work on products that make a tangible impact. It's not just a job; it's an opportunity to shape experiences for millions of users. If you're willing to learn, adapt, and embrace the mindset of continuous improvement, QA could be the perfect fit. By weighing the pros and cons honestly, you'll set yourself up to not just enter this field but thrive in it.

The Career Change Mindset

Overcoming Self-Doubt

Making a career change can feel like standing at the base of a mountain, staring up at the climb ahead. The thought of starting from scratch is enough to make anyone hesitate. "What if I'm too old to learn this?" "What if I fail?" These are the voices of self-doubt, and trust me, they're normal. Everyone who's ever made a big shift has wrestled with them. But here's the truth: you're not starting from scratch; you're starting from experience. The skills you've honed in your current or previous roles—problem-solving, communication, attention to detail—are the foundation you'll build on in QA.

Look at people who've successfully navigated career changes. You'll find teachers who became developers, chefs who turned into UX designers, and stay-at-home parents who found their niche in tech. They didn't succeed because they were fearless; they succeeded because they embraced the learning curve and stayed committed. They leaned into their transferable skills and realized that what seemed like unrelated experiences were actually assets in their new careers.

Preparation is your best tool for quieting those doubts. When you start to understand the basics of QA, like testing methodologies or common tools, you'll feel the shift. Knowledge breeds confidence. Each time you grasp a new concept or complete a hands-on project, it's like putting another piece into the puzzle. Doubts don't disappear overnight, but with each step forward, they lose their power. That's how you conquer the mountain—one steady step at a time.

Setting Realistic Expectations

Breaking into QA isn't something that happens overnight. It's going to require a combination of effort, focus, and consistency. Some people take weeks, others take months, depending on how much time you can dedicate. Think of it like learning a new sport. You start with the basics—getting your stance right, understanding the rules—and then move on to more complex techniques. The key is to stay patient with yourself and keep showing up.

Shifting into a QA career is an exciting move, but it's important to approach it with your eyes wide open. There's a learning curve, and understanding that from the start can save you a lot of frustration. You're entering a field with its own tools, terminology, and workflows, and while some concepts might click immediately, others will take time to sink in. That's not a sign you're failing; it's just part of the process.

One of the best strategies is to start small. Focus on one thing at a time: learn a testing methodology, explore a tool like Jira, or complete a small online course. Each small step you take builds momentum. It's easy to get overwhelmed if you think you need to master everything at once, but the truth is, mastery comes from repetition and layering your knowledge over time. Give yourself permission to be a beginner, and before long, you'll look back and realize just how far you've come.

Leveraging Your Background

One of the biggest misconceptions about changing careers is that you're starting from scratch. You're not. You're bringing a lifetime of skills, experience, and perspective to the table, and that's your secret weapon. Think about the skills you've honed in your current field—problem-solving, teamwork, communication, or attention to detail. These aren't just soft skills; they're the foundation of a successful career in QA. If you've ever worked under tight deadlines, managed competing priorities, or navigated tricky client relationships, you already have what it takes to excel in this field.

Your industry background, no matter what it is, can also be an asset. Let's say you've worked in healthcare, retail, or education. QA exists in every industry that relies on software, and having domain knowledge gives you an edge. You already understand the workflows, the pain points, and the needs of end users, which makes you uniquely qualified to identify what works and what doesn't. Instead of seeing your previous career as unrelated, frame it as the perfect stepping stone.

Even the challenges you've faced along the way are opportunities in disguise. If you've ever had to pivot or learn something completely new, that resilience will serve you well here. QA is all about adapting, troubleshooting, and continuously improving. By leveraging what you already know and reframing your past experiences as strengths, you're not just making a career change—you're building on a foundation that's already solid.

3

Chapter 2: Acquiring QA Knowledge and Skills

Learning the Fundamentals of QA

Understanding Software Development Life Cycles (SDLC and STLC)

When you're stepping into the world of QA, understanding the bigger picture of software development is like getting a backstage pass to how the magic happens. Every piece of software, from the simplest app to the most complex system, follows a process to go from idea to reality. That's the Software Development Life Cycle, or SDLC, in a nutshell. It's the roadmap developers follow to ensure their ideas become functional, polished products. QA fits into this journey as the safety net, ensuring nothing slips through the cracks.

Different companies use different approaches, and each one has its own rhythm. Agile, for instance, is all about speed and collaboration, with work happening in short sprints. QA plays a dynamic role here, testing as the product evolves. Waterfall is more traditional, with a linear progression, and QA typically swoops in at the end to validate the finished product. Then there's DevOps, which is all about blending development and operations for faster delivery. QA here focuses on automation and continuous testing to keep things moving seamlessly.

To do your job well, you'll also need to understand the types of testing that exist. Functional testing ensures the software does what it's supposed to. Performance testing checks if it can handle pressure. Security testing ensures safety. Each type serves a purpose, and knowing which to use when is part of mastering your craft. Once you grasp these basics, you'll start to see the flow of how development and QA work hand in hand.

Key QA Concepts and Tools

At the heart of QA are two essential approaches: manual testing and automated testing. Think of manual testing as the art of putting yourself in the user's shoes, exploring the software step by step to find bugs. It's hands-on and intuitive, making it ideal for catching those quirky, one-off issues that automation might miss. Automated testing, on the other hand, is like setting up a robot to do the repetitive tasks for you. It's efficient, precise, and especially powerful when testing large systems or running the same checks over and over. Both methods have their strengths, and learning when to use each is a game-changer.

Then there are the tools, the bread and butter of any QA professional. Selenium is a big name in automation—it's open-source, versatile, and perfect for automating web applications. JIRA is a go-to for tracking bugs and managing workflows; it's where you'll keep tabs on what's been tested and what still needs attention. TestRail helps you organize and track test cases, ensuring you don't miss a step in your testing process. These tools might seem intimidating at first, but once you start using them, they quickly become second nature.

Speaking of test cases, this is where the real magic happens. Writing a test case is like creating a recipe for how to test a specific feature. You define what to test, the steps to follow, and the expected outcome. It's a skill that takes practice, but once you've got it down, it sets the foundation for everything else in QA.

Beginner-Friendly Learning Resources

Diving into QA is a lot easier when you know where to find the right resources. Online courses and certification programs are a great starting point. One of the most recognized is the ISTQB certification, which gives you a solid foundation in QA principles and looks great on a resume. Platforms like Udemy, Coursera, and LinkedIn Learning are packed with beginner-friendly courses, letting you dip your toes into testing methods, tools, and strategies without feeling overwhelmed. The best part? You can move at your own pace, whether you're squeezing in lessons after work or dedicating weekends to it.

Books and blogs are another goldmine. Authors like Cem Kaner, who wrote *Testing Computer Software*, break down complex concepts into digestible chunks, making them perfect for newcomers. QA forums and blogs offer real-world insights straight from professionals in the field. Websites like SoftwareTestingHelp and TestAutomationGuru are filled with tips, tutorials, and troubleshooting guides that can answer the "How do I actually do this?" questions that inevitably pop up.

Finding a mentor can also be transformative. A seasoned QA professional can guide you, share their experiences, and help you avoid common pitfalls. If you don't have a direct connection, QA boot camps often come with built-in mentorship and hands-on projects to build your skills and confidence. You don't have to learn everything at once. With the right resources, the path becomes clearer, and each step forward feels like progress toward something exciting.

Hands-On Practice

Creating a Test Environment

When it comes to learning QA, theory can only take you so far. The real growth happens when you roll up your sleeves and start practicing. Luckily, you don't need a fancy setup or expensive software to get started. Many tools, like Selenium and Postman, offer free versions that are perfect for beginners. These tools let you experiment with creating automated tests, exploring APIs, or simply understanding how testing fits into the bigger picture of software development.

One of the easiest ways to dive in is by downloading demo applications specifically designed for testing. These apps are built to simulate real-world scenarios, complete with bugs and challenges for you to uncover. They're like your personal QA playground, where you can practice writing test cases, executing tests, and even exploring different types of testing like functionality or usability. A quick search will lead you to plenty of options, and they're a fantastic way to build confidence while developing your skills.

As you practice, consider creating a project you can showcase in a portfolio. This could be as simple as documenting your testing process for a demo app or as involved as automating a series of tests on a small application. The goal is to have something tangible that demonstrates your abilities to potential employers. It doesn't need to be perfect; it just needs to show that you're proactive, curious, and capable of applying what you've learned. That's the kind of practice that opens doors.

Building a Portfolio

Your portfolio is more than just a collection of your work—it's your chance to tell a story about your journey into QA. Start by documenting your test cases, bug reports, and test plans. These are the bread and butter of QA, and showing that you can create clear, thorough documentation speaks volumes about your skills. Treat it like a behind-the-scenes look at your thought process, where you explain not only what you did but why you did it. Employers love seeing that kind of insight.

Once you've built something you're proud of, share it. GitHub is a great platform for showcasing your projects. Even if you're new to coding, you can upload test scripts or summaries of your manual testing efforts. If GitHub feels too technical, consider creating a simple personal website. It doesn't have to be fancy—just a place where you can neatly organize and present your work. It's about making it easy for someone to see what you bring to the table.

Finally, don't overlook certifications and the effort you've put into learning. Add those achievements to your portfolio alongside any projects. They show a commitment to growth and a willingness to put in the time to improve. Your portfolio doesn't need to be perfect or packed with years of experience; it just needs to reflect your unique journey and the value you can bring to a QA team. When done right, it becomes a powerful tool for opening doors in your new career.

Overcoming Challenges in Learning QA

Let's face it—learning something new isn't always smooth sailing. There will be moments when you feel stuck, overwhelmed, or unsure if you're even moving in the right direction. That's normal. The key is learning how to push through those challenges without losing momentum. Staying motivated starts with setting realistic expectations. You're not going to master QA overnight, and that's okay. Focus on small, consistent wins. Instead of trying to automate an entire application, start by automating one simple test. Each small success builds your confidence and keeps the process manageable.

When technical problems arise—and they will—remember you're not alone. The QA community is full of people who've been exactly where you are. Online forums like StackOverflow or QA-specific groups on LinkedIn are goldmines for finding answers and learning from others' experiences. Don't be afraid to ask questions, even if you think they're basic. The only bad question is the one you didn't ask.

Consistency is your greatest ally. It's better to practice a little every day than to cram everything into a single marathon session. Pick one small task—writing a test case, exploring a new tool, or reading up on a testing concept—and commit to it daily. Over time, these small efforts compound into real, tangible skills. The challenges you face are opportunities to grow. Each hurdle you overcome is proof that you're not just learning QA—you're becoming resilient, resourceful, and ready for what's next.

4

Chapter 3: Landing Your First QA Job

Preparing to Apply

Crafting a Winning Resume and Cover Letter

Your resume and cover letter are your first chance to make an impression, so they need to do more than list your past jobs—they need to tell your story. For someone transitioning into QA, the magic lies in highlighting transferable skills and tying them to what the role requires. Think about the problem-solving you've done in previous jobs or the detail-oriented nature of tasks you've mastered. Whether you've managed workflows, analyzed data, or organized projects, frame those experiences in a way that shows you're already thinking like a QA professional.

Tailoring your applications to specific roles is the secret sauce. Instead of sending out the same resume to every opening, take a few minutes to understand what each company is looking for. If they mention test automation, weave in the online course you took on Selenium or the automation scripts you practiced. If they value teamwork, spotlight a project where collaboration led to success. This targeted approach immediately makes you stand out.

It's easy to fall into common resume traps like cramming too much information or using vague buzzwords. Avoid phrases like "team player" unless you back them up with examples. Keep it clean, focused, and easy to skim. Employers don't need your life story—they need to know how you'll add value to their team. Think of your resume and cover letter as a conversation starter, one that leaves them curious and eager to learn more about what you bring to the table.

Building a Professional Network

One of the most overlooked but powerful tools in landing your first QA job is the network you build along the way. When you're just starting out, it can feel intimidating to connect with people who already seem light-years ahead of you in their careers. But here's the thing: most people love sharing what they know, especially with someone genuinely eager to learn. Joining QA communities and forums is an easy first step. These spaces are filled with professionals at every stage of their journey, and they're often more supportive than you'd expect. Asking questions, sharing your learning experiences, or even just observing the conversations can make you feel like part of the tribe.

LinkedIn can be a goldmine if you use it well. It's not just about sending random connection requests; it's about engaging. Follow QA professionals, comment on their posts, and share updates about your own progress. If someone's career inspires you, send them a thoughtful message. Something as simple as, "I'm new to QA and learning a lot. Your post about test automation really resonated—thank you!" can open doors to meaningful connections.

Don't underestimate the value of live interaction, either. QA meetups and webinars are where you can put faces to names and make an impression. Even if you're nervous, showing up says a lot about your commitment. Networking isn't about knowing the most people—it's about creating genuine relationships. Those connections can lead to advice, mentorship, and, sometimes, the exact opportunity you've been looking for.

Creating a Strategic Job Search Plan

Looking for a QA job can feel overwhelming at first, but having a game plan turns chaos into focus. The first step is identifying roles that align with where you are right now. As someone new to the field, aim for beginner-friendly positions like QA tester, junior QA analyst, or manual tester. These roles often focus on the foundational skills you've been building and can act as a springboard for growth. The key is to find opportunities where you can hit the ground running while still having room to learn.

Job boards are an obvious choice, but they're only as effective as your approach. Instead of passively scrolling through listings, be intentional. Use keywords that match your experience and training, like "entry-level QA" or "manual testing." Filter results to focus on industries or locations that resonate with you. When you find a role, don't just skim the description—analyze it. Tailor your resume and application to align with what the company is seeking.

Once you start applying, staying organized is critical. Track each application with details like the company name, role, date submitted, and whether you've followed up. Following up is where many candidates drop the ball, but it's often where magic happens. A simple, polite email checking on the status of your application can remind a recruiter of your interest and keep you on their radar. A strategic job search plan isn't just about finding openings—it's about making sure those openings lead to interviews, and ultimately, offers.

Nailing the Interview

Common QA Interview Questions

The interview is your chance to showcase your skills, personality, and passion for QA. When it comes to technical questions, you can expect problem-solving scenarios that test your ability to think critically. Don't panic if you don't have the perfect answer right away. Interviewers want to see how you approach challenges. Take your time to walk them through your thought process. If you're asked about how you'd test a feature, talk about the steps you'd take, the tools you might use, and the factors you'd consider—whether it's manual testing or automation. If you get stuck, be honest and explain how you'd find a solution, whether that's through research, collaboration, or experimenting.

Behavioral questions are often used to gauge how you handle real-world situations. You might be asked how you've worked under pressure or how you've resolved conflicts. For these, use the STAR method—Situation, Task, Action, Result. Be specific about the challenges you've faced and how you've navigated them, even if they're from a different industry or role. The key is showing that your problem-solving and interpersonal skills are transferable to QA.

When explaining your career transition, approach it with confidence. Frame your past experiences as assets that will make you a strong asset in your new QA role. Whether you've honed attention to detail, learned to work in teams, or embraced continuous learning, these are all qualities that make you the right fit for QA. Remember, confidence is contagious. Own your journey and show how it's led you to this exciting next step.

Showcasing Your Portfolio

When it comes to standing out in a QA interview, your portfolio is one of your most powerful assets. It's concrete proof of your skills and dedication, and it can make all the difference. One of the best ways to showcase your abilities is by presenting well-documented test cases and bug reports. Walk the interviewer through a few of your best examples—be it manual testing, functional testing, or even exploratory testing. Show them how you structured your test cases, the steps you followed, and how you documented the results. Explain any challenges you encountered and how you resolved them. This not only demonstrates your technical ability but also your attention to detail and thoroughness, qualities highly valued in QA.

Another key element is demonstrating the tools and

techniques you've mastered. Whether it's test management tools like JIRA, test automation frameworks like Selenium, or even simple spreadsheets, showing that you can use industry-standard tools with confidence is crucial. You don't have to be an expert in everything, but a basic understanding of these tools and how they fit into the workflow will go a long way in impressing your interviewer.

Lastly, don't forget to highlight your learning process and growth mindset. QA is all about continuous improvement, so let your interviewers know how you've grown, how you keep learning, and how you plan to continue evolving. Talk about the resources you've used—online courses, forums, or mentors—and how those have shaped your journey. This tells interviewers you're committed to being the best QA professional you can be.

Post-Interview Strategies

Once the interview is over, the work doesn't stop. In fact, the post-interview phase is just as important as what happened during the meeting. First, send a personalized thank-you note. Keep it simple but sincere—thank them for their time, express your enthusiasm for the role, and briefly reiterate why you're the right fit. This gesture not only shows your professionalism but also gives you one last chance to leave a positive impression. It's a small touch that can make you stand out from other candidates.

Next, take some time to reflect on the interview itself. What went well? What could you have done differently? This process helps you fine-tune your approach for future interviews. Maybe you noticed you could explain a technical concept more clearly, or perhaps you felt a particular question caught you off guard. These are all learning opportunities that will make you more prepared next time. The more you analyze and learn from each interview, the better you'll become at handling the next one.

Finally, if you receive an offer, approach the negotiation process professionally. Don't be afraid to ask questions or clarify details, but do it respectfully. This is your chance to ensure the terms are aligned with your expectations and market value. Whether it's salary, benefits, or work schedule, take your time to evaluate the offer before making a decision. Negotiation doesn't have to be intimidating—it's a conversation, not a confrontation.

5

Chapter 4: Growing into a QA Manager Role

Excelling in Your First QA Job

Learning on the Job

Landing your first QA role is just the beginning. The real growth happens once you're in the trenches, navigating real projects and challenges. One of the most important things you can do is fully immerse yourself in mastering the tools and methodologies your team uses. Theoretical knowledge is great, but applying it in a live environment is a different game. Don't be afraid to dive in—experiment, ask questions, and take detailed notes. Every test case, every bug report, and every tool you explore deepens your understanding and makes you sharper.

Feedback is your secret weapon for growth. Seek it out actively from peers, supervisors, and even developers. Constructive criticism isn't personal; it's a roadmap for improvement.

Approach feedback sessions with an open mind and a hunger to learn. Reflect on the insights you receive and apply them to your daily work. Small, consistent improvements add up faster than you think.

Understanding team dynamics is another crucial piece of the puzzle. QA isn't a solo sport. You're collaborating with developers, project managers, and sometimes even clients. Learning how to communicate effectively, navigate different personalities, and contribute positively to the team culture will set you apart. Observe how seasoned colleagues handle tricky situations or tight deadlines and adapt those lessons to your own style. Growth in QA is as much about technical skills as it is about becoming a team player who adds value at every turn.

Building a Reputation for Excellence

In QA, your reputation is everything. It's the currency you trade on, the invisible badge that opens doors to new opportunities. Delivering consistent, high-quality work is the foundation. Every test case you write, every bug you document, and every report you submit is a reflection of your standards. Attention to detail isn't just a buzzword here—it's your secret weapon. Take the extra moment to double-check. Catch what others miss. When your work consistently exceeds expectations, you build trust, and that trust becomes your professional calling card.

Initiative is what separates top performers from the pack. Don't just wait for tasks to land in your inbox. Look for gaps in processes. If you see something that could be streamlined, speak up. If a project is struggling, volunteer to troubleshoot.

The best QA professionals aren't just problem solvers—they're problem seekers. They anticipate issues before they escalate. Taking initiative doesn't mean being a know-it-all; it means being the person who steps up, quietly and confidently, when things need fixing.

Networking might seem like an afterthought, but it's a career accelerator. Start within your team. Build genuine connections with developers, project managers, and other QA members. Understanding their challenges makes collaboration smoother and more productive. Outside your company, engage with the QA community. Attend webinars, join forums, and connect on LinkedIn. These relationships offer fresh perspectives and often lead to unexpected opportunities. Excellence isn't just about what you know—it's about who knows you and what you stand for.

Setting Long-Term Career Goals

Stepping into your first QA role is just the beginning—think of it as the first chapter in a much longer story. To make this a bestseller, you need a vision for where you're headed. Start by identifying areas of specialization that resonate with you. Maybe you're fascinated by automation testing, or perhaps performance testing sparks your curiosity. Dive deep into what excites you. Specialization doesn't mean limiting yourself; it means becoming so good at one thing that opportunities naturally find you.

Certifications aren't just pieces of paper—they're proof that you've invested in yourself. Look into industry-recognized programs like ISTQB, or advanced ones if you're aiming higher. Each certification adds credibility to your name and sharpens your skills. But don't stop there. Think about roles beyond the current horizon. Advanced roles like QA Lead or QA Architect aren't mythical titles reserved for a select few. They're milestones on your roadmap.

Mapping your path to QA management starts with understanding what great managers do. Observe the leaders around you. How do they handle challenges? How do they communicate with their teams? Leadership isn't about knowing all the answers; it's about guiding others to find them. Set small, achievable goals along the way. Maybe it's leading a project or mentoring a junior colleague. These steps build the foundation for bigger moves. Success in QA isn't a sprint—it's a series of intentional strides toward mastery and influence.

Developing Leadership Skills

Becoming a Mentor

Stepping into mentorship might feel like you're not ready—like you need to hit some magical milestone before guiding others. Here's the truth: You're ready right now. Sharing knowledge with junior QA professionals doesn't require you to know everything; it requires you to share what you know. Think back to when you started. What were the gaps you struggled to fill? What advice would have made your journey smoother? Passing those insights on doesn't just help others—it reinforces your own learning.

Organizing team training sessions and workshops might sound intimidating, but it's one of the most powerful ways to grow. Start small. Pick a tool or technique you've mastered and break it down for others. Create a space where questions are welcome, and mistakes are seen as part of the process. Not only does this build your credibility, but it also shifts you from being seen as a contributor to a leader. You're not just doing the work; you're elevating the whole team.

Your personal success stories are more than just tales—they're fuel. When you share how you overcame challenges, it's not about bragging. It's about showing others what's possible. People connect with stories, especially the ones that involve struggle and growth. By opening up about your journey, you're not just inspiring others—you're building a culture of resilience and ambition. Mentorship isn't a one-way street. As you help others rise, you'll find yourself rising too.

Improving Team Collaboration

In the world of QA, you're often the glue that holds cross-functional teams together. Managing these diverse groups—developers, designers, product managers—requires more than just technical know-how. It's about understanding people. Start by listening more than you speak. What are their goals? Where do they feel stuck? When you understand their perspectives, you can align QA objectives with the bigger picture, turning potential friction points into collaborative opportunities.

Conflicts are inevitable, but they're also growth moments in disguise. When tensions rise, resist the urge to avoid them. Address issues head-on, but stay neutral. Focus on the problem, not the people. Encourage open dialogue, and guide the team toward solutions that serve everyone. Remember, a positive environment isn't about eliminating challenges; it's about creating a space where challenges are tackled with respect and transparency.

Advocating for QA best practices across departments is where you transform from a team player to a leader. Don't just tell others what needs to be done—show them why it matters. Share real-world examples of how quality processes have saved projects or boosted customer satisfaction. Be the person who bridges the gap between QA and other teams, speaking their language while standing firm on the principles of quality. When you become the advocate who makes everyone else's job easier, you're not just improving collaboration; you're elevating the entire organization's game.

Building Strategic Vision

To thrive as a QA leader, you need to see beyond bug reports and sprint cycles. Strategic vision starts with understanding how your role fits into the larger mission of the company. Ask yourself: How does QA contribute to long-term business goals? The answers will guide you in contributing to company-wide quality initiatives that move the needle. Whether it's enhancing customer satisfaction metrics or reducing deployment times, tie your QA efforts to measurable outcomes.

Process improvement isn't about making incremental tweaks; it's about identifying game-changing opportunities. Look for patterns—recurring bottlenecks, common points of failure, areas where communication breaks down. Then, propose solutions that don't just fix the problem but prevent it from recurring. Maybe it's automating a manual process, introducing a new tool, or refining testing protocols. Every improvement should serve a dual purpose: boosting efficiency and elevating quality standards.

Preparing to lead QA teams and projects means stepping out of your comfort zone. Volunteer for initiatives outside your immediate responsibilities. Take the lead on cross-departmental projects, even if they seem daunting. This isn't about proving yourself—it's about learning what leadership feels like in real time. Pay attention to what works, what doesn't, and how you can bring out the best in others. When you align your day-to-day actions with a broader vision, you're not just managing QA—you're shaping the future of the company's quality culture.

Stepping into QA Management

The Transition to Management

Moving from QA specialist to manager is like stepping from the lab onto the bridge of a ship. Suddenly, your role expands beyond finding bugs; you're navigating teams and steering projects. Balancing technical know-how with managerial duties is the first hurdle. The trick? Never lose touch with the work. Stay sharp on the tools and methods your team uses but resist micromanaging. Your value now lies in guiding others, not doing it all yourself. Think of it as shifting from player to coach—you don't have to score every goal, but you need to know the game inside out.

Delegation isn't about offloading tasks; it's about empowering your team. Identify strengths and assign tasks accordingly.

Trust your people and give them room to grow. Micromanaging will burn you out and frustrate them. Instead, set clear expectations and let them take ownership. Check in, offer support, and celebrate wins, but don't hover. Effective delegation turns individual contributors into a cohesive, self-sufficient unit.

Strategic decision-making is where you prove your mettle. Every choice impacts the team and the product, so zoom out and see the bigger picture. Weigh short-term fixes against long-term goals. Ask yourself: Will this improve quality and efficiency in the long run? Embrace tough calls—they're part of the job. The best managers aren't afraid to make bold moves when needed. As you settle into this role, remember that leadership isn't about control; it's about setting a direction and inspiring others to follow.

Managing QA Teams

Managing a QA team is like curating a band—you need the right mix of talent, direction, and harmony. Hiring is your first critical move. Don't just look for resumes that tick boxes. Seek out curious minds who ask great questions and demonstrate a hunger for learning. Technical skills can be taught; the right mindset is gold. Once you've got them, onboarding sets the tone. Immerse new hires in your culture and processes early. Pair them with mentors, introduce them to real projects, and make sure they understand that quality isn't just about finding bugs—it's about ownership and excellence.

Setting team goals isn't just a box-ticking exercise. Align individual aspirations with broader business objectives. Clear, measurable targets give everyone direction and a sense of purpose. Regular check-ins, not just annual reviews, keep the momentum going. Evaluate performance through progress, not perfection. Celebrate small wins and use setbacks as teaching moments.

Culture is where it all comes together. Foster an environment where quality isn't an afterthought—it's the default. Create accountability by leading from the front; demonstrate the standards you expect. Encourage open feedback loops where mistakes are learning opportunities, not failures. When team members feel safe to take risks and share ideas, you'll see innovation skyrocket. Remember, a great QA team doesn't just catch issues—they prevent them, solve them, and continuously improve the game.

Future-Proofing Your Career

Future-proofing your QA career isn't just about survival—it's about staying ahead of the curve and setting the standard. Technology evolves at breakneck speed, and QA is no exception. Staying updated on emerging trends like AI-driven testing, continuous integration, and new automation tools is non-negotiable. Subscribe to industry newsletters, follow thought leaders, and dive into tech blogs. The goal is to anticipate shifts, not react to them.

Expanding your skill set is your secret weapon. Certifications like advanced ISTQB levels or specialized ones in automation or security testing aren't just resume fillers—they open doors. They challenge you to grow and position you as a top-tier candidate. More importantly, they signal to others (and yourself) that you're committed to excellence.

Building a personal brand is where you go from participant to leader. Share your insights on LinkedIn, contribute to QA forums, or start a blog about your experiences. Speak at webinars or local meetups. The more you share, the more you learn, and the more you become known as someone worth listening to. Thought leaders aren't people with all the answers—they're the ones asking the right questions and pushing the conversation forward.

Remember, the future belongs to those who don't just adapt but drive change. Stay curious, stay visible, and keep investing in your own evolution. The payoff? A career that's not just future-proof but future-leading.

6

Conclusion

Making a career change can be daunting, but "Landing Your First QA Job" is here to guide you through every step of the journey. If you're contemplating transitioning into Quality Assurance, reading this book before taking the plunge is essential. It lays the foundation for understanding the industry, its tools, and how to position yourself for success. Whether you're uncertain about the skills required or overwhelmed by the thought of entering a new field, this book has armed you with the knowledge and practical advice to make a smooth and informed transition.

Throughout the book, we've covered key concepts of QA, from understanding the software development life-cycle to diving into the tools and methods used in the industry. You've learned how to build a strong portfolio, network effectively, and master the art of interviews. The book also helped you set realistic expectations, develop a growth mindset, and plan for long-term success. Each chapter is designed to keep you focused, motivated, and well-equipped to land that first QA job.

Thank you for reading all the way to the end! Your commitment to learning and growth is truly commendable. If this book has helped you in any way, I'd really appreciate it if you could leave a review on Amazon. Your feedback not only helps me improve, but it also helps other aspiring QA professionals find the guidance they need to succeed.

I wish you the best of luck on your career journey and hope you achieve great things in the world of QA!

References

12 Quality Assurance Training Courses for beginners. (n.d.). SC Training (Formerly EdApp) Microlearning Programs. https://training.safetyculture.com/10-quality-assurance-training-courses/

Admin. (2024, January 5). *Why should you choose QA as your career?* Best Software Training Institute - Online | Corporate | Weekend. https://qatraininghub.com/why-choose-qa-as-your-career/

Sharma, I. (2024, August 30). *SDLC vs STLC: What is the Difference?* Software and Technology Blog - TatvaSoft. https://www.tatvasoft.com/outsourcing/2022/08/sdlc-vs-stlc.html

www.ingramcontent.com/pod-product-compliance
Lightning Source LLC
Chambersburg PA
CBHW070943220526
45469CB00007B/2496